Introduction

Hi, my name is Linus Ocasio. I have been in the entrepreneur world over a decade now. This book is for any new person or group wanting to start a business or any existing business no matter the size who wants the truth about how to grow and scale their business through sales and marketing. As you can tell, by the title, I am direct and to the point. No fake it until you make it, just be straight up. If you are not a person who tells it like it is, or even open to listen to someone who tells it like it is, this book is not for you so put the book back on the shelf or search another title. But if your someone or a business ready to take it to the next level, this book is for you. I have spent an enormous amount of money figuring out what marketing and sales outlets and tactics works best. So, let's just say you are riding off my money. You will not get all details the details of how each category of this book. The point of this book is to tell you what my professional perspective is regarding different areas of sales and marketing facets. At the end of this book, you should have a clear understanding that marketing is an outgoing and changing part of business. One thing that works now, may not work two months from now. Maybe slow seasons may require you to vamp up your internet marketing versus magazine. Yes, I wrote this book to make money, but I only write about things I am passionate about. I want YOU to WIN. When you read this book, you will know what you need to do. I'm going to tell you in a short book what works and doesn't work. Cut all the BullShit and guessing games and start making more money. If you need any help, throughout the book and at the end will be resources to get started.

Starting Your Own Business

If you are ready thins books and want to start your own business, this section is very vital to the foundation of your company and future success. There are so many variables that go into growing a company into a fruitful entity. But for the sake of this book we are on the topic of sales and marketing. So, when starting a business there are really two personalities that you will fall into. You will either be the type to grow, get out there, mess up, learn the process and close deals and the second is you are the person who wants better, but doesn't really want to deal with people or get out there and get the job done. The type of personality will determine what marketing factors will be the most efficient for you in the beginning.

Scenario 1 – Go getter and Social Butterfly

If your someone who loves talking to people, well you have a definite advantage over someone who doesn't. With a strong work ethic and commitment to grow, the possibilities are high. If your someone who has a big budget for marketing, combine it with a strong work ethic and ability to cold prospect the future looks bright

Scenario 2 – Are you going to buy? If NOT, don't bother me

On the other hand, if you're not a people person, you **MUST** have a budget to hire sales people, market online, magazines, billboards, radio, etc. My wife is a businesswoman, she has an online e-commerce business. She doesn't have to deal with consumers face to face. They either buy or don't buy. She loves it that way. She is a to herself family woman. She doesn't have, not care to want to have patience with difficult consumers. In my time in business, I have realized that just because someone is in business doesn't mean they are great with people or nice. If that is your personality, this is a cold hard truth.

Hiring Sales People

Imagine having that hot shot salesperson that you see in all the Hollywood movies who close deals left and right effortlessly. Let's **CUT THE BULLSHIT.** Here is another cold truth, the chances of finding that dream salesperson is like hitting the Mega-lottery. This has always been the most aggravating part of business. I have hired dozens of sales people who say they are all in and don't ever produce to the extent that they claimed in interviews. You see, a true sales person will not be so focused on the base, but more on the commission structure.

I remembered, I hired close friends to do a job, that they really were not cut out to do, no matter what they say they will do. There was another time I hired this saleswoman who was so focused on the base more than the commission. This is a red flag, because true sales people are focused on the bigger vision. There was a lady that begged me to hire her, and she sold me on all the things she can do. So, I signed her, and a few weeks later, no results. My wife is the toughest person to sell, she has her own beliefs about most people are full of SHIT, but she has firsthand witnessed the BULLSHIT EXCUSES people give me. There was another saleslady that sold my wife and I on her goals and what she could do for my company. We called all her references, everything checked out well, and then she just disappeared a few weeks later. I mean who doesn't come to collect their check and answer their boss.

Then there was this man in his mid-50's who was a fire cracker. I walked into a well-known coffee shop, go figure out what that is, when suddenly, I hear a gentleman say, "Man that is an awesome shirt." I was wearing my church shirt. He was a man a faith who was one of the biggest producers at one of the largest pharmaceutical companies in the world. We met and hat and I started to pay him weekly. I watched him over the weeks, he kept a sharp work logged, tracked his mileage, turned in all his gas receipts, gave me his CRM at the end of each business day. But after a few weeks of not closing, he started to come up with excuses. It amazes me who peoples energy change in such a short period of time. The reality is no one will care about your dreams and goals except those few in our life and YOU.

I didn't recruit the best sales people until I grew my company strong enough and could afford them. First you must find that person. Most salespeople are average and they talk a good game, but won't have ability to close enough business for you to thrive. The reality is, anyone that good, you better have the budget, compensation plan, and vision, for them to even consider coming to your company. So where am I getting at, you're probably wondering. Here it is, you will be out of business if your business is going to be dependent on that dream salesperson. You need to be that dream salesperson first, and/or have a great marketing company who can drive your business until you make enough to pull in a great salesperson. Moral of this section is, do not trust salespeople to build your business in the beginning.

Realities of business

It sounds ideal where everyone tells you yes and the stars and planets line up for you. But let's **CUT THE BULLSHIT.** Unfortunately, that's not most people's case. You are going to get so many more **NO's, maybe's and I'll think about it** (which is a kind and fake way to tell you no). See in business it's either **YES** or **NO.** Anything beyond that is **BULLSHIT!** If you were to meet me, I would tell you straight up if I can get involved or not. I remember being pool side with a billionaire when I won a company trip when I was in the investment industry. After he chatted with a few people, I went up to him with my little sister just to talk because we all played basketball. But I remember one key thing he said, "Linus, if you can remember this one thing and apply it, you will always do well. **THE WORLD IS NOTHING BUT A NUMBERS GAME**, it is the most profound SHIT, I have ever thought of, you have the problem and solution in the same DAMN sentence." I have applied that to everything I have ever done. So, want to know how you combat all the **NO's** to get to all the **YES's**? This is what I do to get results, I do over 100 new contacts a day at least 6 days a week. You MUST **CRANK OUT MASSIVE** numbers in a **SHORT** period of **TIME.** Anything less than that will result in **SKEWED** and **MEDIOCRE RESULTS.** I believe in the Wall Street Bull, it represents being optimistic and pushing your way to prosperity. I pound the pavement until I see results. One thing I recommend is not caring about what anyone thinks. So many people will doubt you or not believe in your product or service. I believe any product can sell with the right marketing. But ensure you are willing to change and ask for help when needed.

Internet Marketing

Welcome to the present age, where internet is everything. As a new or existing business, your online presence better be off the chain. There is so many dynamics and variables that go into having a strong online presence. From SEO, to Ad words, to e-mail marketing, Geo- fencing and much more. In this world, the bigger your database and presence online, the greater your revenue will grow.

I have seen so many businesses with great products and services go by the waste side, stay average, and even go out of business because they couldn't stay competitive. I remember talking to this business owner about why they should be marketing heavily on the internet, and they said they didn't need to because they had a great location and he was doing some small ads in some local coupon books. A few months later, as I was in route to a client, I see his company went out of business.

What can we learn from this former business owner. A great location doesn't always correlate with great success. In today's age, if someone wants to spend their money, they are going to search it online. Did you know that most people search and whatever they see come up at the top of their search on the first page, that is who they will most likely do business with. The top three websites in any given location and key words will always get 100% of clicks of people who search.

SEO

You probably heard the acronym SEO. You're probably asking yourself, "What is SEO?" It stands for search engine optimization. On the internet, you want to build a strong SEO website so that your website has authority and can organically come up at the top of your industries most searched key words. If that is something you are interested in, all the resource information will be at the end of this book.

Ad Words

Ad words is for people and businesses that do not want to spend the time and are impatient to build their sites credibility. When you pay with ad words you get to be at the top of searches with the side logo that says ads. You ever see those links that says ad, that is an example. One of my current client that pays my company thousands of dollars a month for each location because ad words works for them.

E-mail Marketing

E-mail marketing and campaigns are awesome to send a quick notice of specials you have in one easy template. Image reaching thousands or more with the click of one button. These are awesome for client and customer engagements and Call to Action campaigns. By the way join our e-mail list on my website for latest news, events, tips, and discounts.

Visibility-Engine

This is probably the most awesome program I have ever seen for internet marketing and revenue growth. Most businesses do not have this program and I am proud to be a part of this proprietary program. We can identify the 3% ready and willing buyers for your products in real-time. What if you can reach your consumers before they have the chance at being your competitor's client? Wouldn't you want to explore that possibility? If you want to totally change the trajectory of your business, contact Drew www.internetservicesgroup.net/visibility-engine and e-mail Drew@spgx.net

Here is a list of things you can do marketing wise within internet marketing

- Local SEO
- Mobile Phone Voice Mail drop – ** New!
- Video creation and promotion
- Email marketing
- Copywriting
- Autoresponders
- Press releases
- Email lists – sale or rent
- Direct Mail
- Mobile App development
- Reputation management (Maintain or repair)
- Social media management
- Instagram
- Facebook
- Twitter
- Linked In
- more…
- Classified Ads – Craigslist, Back page
- Link Building
- List Building
- List Rental
- SEO
- Mobile Ads
- AdWords
- Google Analytics
- Software testing
- Web development
- Web bot development
- Lead generation

Your internet marketing campaign will be tailored to your objectives, budget and product or service. We are committed to long term mutually beneficial partnerships.

Social Media

This day and age most people think they are their own little celebrity. Social media truly allows people to connect at a faster rate than ever before. I will break down simply what industries work better on certain platforms for clients. I didn't use social media to build my business, but it is a great tool depending on your industry. I believe you should connect on social media then create a median to get their attention to meet and network. I have a perfect system for this that my clients get when we consult for them. I want to emphasize; **MOST BUSINESSES SHOULD NOT DEPEND ON SOCIAL MEDIA FOR REVENUE.** For example, in **MOST CASES**, a health and fitness company and online fashion store will do way better in getting customers online than a civil engineer and land surveyor. Do you get the picture, know your placements for your company? Get out there and build connects, get referrals, and use some of the solid marketing tools and avenues I have mentioned.

Text Message Marketing

In today's world, text messaging is normal for business to get done. Whether it is an automated system you use to reach consumers with a special text number or you are reaching out to consumers it is applicable to all businesses trying to grow their reach and customer base. I have closed so many deals by using the same simple too over and over. Consistency is where all your success will come from. The average person opens their text message in about 3 minutes. Talk about cutting the time frame. I have a strategy that will get you in front of many businesses and potential consumers. It works so well, I only teach it to the people I mentor. If you want to learn what I know, invest in yourself and book an appointment to learn.

Magazines

Print ads are still very useful depending on what type of print ad and what type of industry you are in. For example, if you are a restaurant, it may be a great tool to put a special savings in a coupon book. A high-end magazine may be great if your products are catered to a higher affluent market. In my professional business experience magazines are a show a statement maker and nothing more. If you get business out of it, then look at it as a plus. Not really something I would do if you are starting off. Always put a coupon number tracker to know what you are getting on your return on investment (ROI). Most advertising companies are trying to sell you space and not truly concerned with your actual money made from it. So, pick and choose when you do it, maybe its only times of the year when you know business will be slow. If you would like a professional marketing opinion, one of my associate's that I trained or I would gladly, consult with you personally at a lower cost for purchasing this book. We charge $1,000 an hour typically, but for readers of this book, you get a discount of $250 an hour.

Billboards

Billboards are a branding tool. I believe billboards are great once your company becomes well established in your operating areas. I have helped many clients who pay for billboards in their first few months of business save money on cancelling and switching where they market. I remember this physician team opened a new Urgent Care and they were paying $900 a month for 1 billboard and they only got 2 clients over the 3 months they committed to. Which did not justify what they paid. My professional opinion, show off your company when you make it.

Radio and Television

Radio and television is another branding tool. This can be an awesome tool if you have the budget for it. These types of outlets require long campaigns to ensure companies and consumers remember who you are. Getting the right hook or jingle will keep consumers intrigued. Again, I believe this outlet is great for companies that are solvent enough and sustainable. You want to be in front of entertainment outlets.

Display Ad's

Have you ever wondered why you seen an ad online or app of something you like or a place you recently traveled too? Well best believe in isn't by coincidence. Many companies are using cookies and display ads to serve anyone who has visited your site or competitors site. What this means is that companies track people who showed an interest in something and serve them ads when they surf the web on other websites. This is a great compliment to your business once you've grown a bit. I wouldn't recommend it as a starting point for most. Once you have built enough traction this is a great way to keep the momentum going. Remember, this world is moving so fast, people aren't taking the time to check something out like they used to. So, be wise when you choose your outlets and when.

Signage and Vehicle Wraps

If you have a bricks and mortars shop or no location, signage is important. Signage can be building sign, flyers, door-hangers, business cars, vehicle wraps, etc. I believe vehicle wraps is vital to all business. Some people don't want it because it's their personal vehicle, others because they feel someone will come after them. For those that want to grow massively, vehicle wraps or signage decal lettering will help you reach more eyes then you can talk to.

Coffee Shops

If you are truly grinding it out there, you probably should know by now that coffee shops are where business is happening. It is the cheapest way to have a meeting in public and connect with so many potential consumers. I have closed more than 90% of business in coffee shops. I have met so met thousands of people in coffee shops, from college students, average worker, business owners, private investigator, mayors, Senators, and so many other fields. Many of them I have done business with in some form or another. I remember when this 57-year-old man, hit me on social media because he heard of my work through a client I had. We met in San Diego, California and in a 10-minute presentation he wrote me a check for over half a million dollars. I was only 23 at the time and hew bought me breakfast. I closed hundreds of deals and found many great partnerships out of working remotely at a coffee shop. Then I realized a way to start getting people to conversate with me. To learn more, contact us at the end of this book.

Partnerships

To me this is where all the magic happens. The biggest and most successful individuals and businesses collaborate with each other. In my case, I will use a few examples. I have an entire tech company that dedicates part of their business just to my companies. We joint venture on so many projects and make money together. There is another company that we joint ventures that deals with B2B consumers with all types of signage. There is another company we joint ventured on a commercial property for the greater vision.

30,000 view point

The title comes from a business associate I know, who is worth a quarter billion. Here are my beliefs for my companies and myself. I have a strong belief in partnerships and internet marketing first. I believe partnerships is how the greatest companies become more massive every few years. Being at the top of search engines in all possible key words that people would search my companies is critical to sustainability.   Having a great sales and marketing department is truly an art, if you want to win, then be a person open to change and let's start achieving your goals and dreams.

What's the Point?

Here is the true answer. Every advertising account executive is going to sell you why you should pay their company to promote your company. I have seen people work at a magazine and sell print ads and then go to television ads and say that the opposite of what they use to sell. They said print is the best audience, then they say television is the best. I mean what a hypocrite right. But they are looking to make money, even if it may not be in your best interest. So, let's get to the point. Do you want clicks and views, or do you want calls and deals? Sounds like a dumb question, but every advertising outlet is going to sell you their reach or view, etc. I wrote this book to save you thousands of dollars a year on marketing. If you take what I said to heart and apply it, you will see an increase in revenue and growth in your company.

Technique

If you are a salesperson who feels they need to learn more, we can help you with that. Great technique is critical for sales. It is like operating like an elite soldier. Or better yet, a sniper. You must know how to work in situations. Being precise with each customer maybe life or death to your sales department or career. You **MUST** learn how to infiltrate new contacts, get their attention, and work them through the process. Sometimes it will be an immediate close, sometimes it will happen in the near or distant future, but that's okay. If your pipeline is full, you will stay busy.

Listen

If you are a business owner and your sales people are telling you something that they strongly feel will change your business for the better, **LISTEN**. Take the time to sit down and hear them out. I have seen countless times business-owners and top sales managers ignore sales peoples, who stop by their shop, advise just because they are a subordinate to them. Personally, I am the one who got rejected a lot. But as time when on, I forced my way with great skills. If you don't like being rejected, don't do it to others. What if I was the one to walk into your business and you rejected me. You would've lost an awesome opportunity to take your business to levels to new heights. This type of attitude of **PRIDE** will cause companies to stagnate or even decline revenue and future prosperity.

Sustainability

Most companies reinvest their money back into the company, but never think about longevity. What I did was use my profits to purchase stocks of big corporation's overtime. The dividends from the big blue-chip companies and other investments I used to pay for my advertisements and marketing. So, I could be more competitive and sustainable because I knew most other businesses are spending their revenue and profits to market. Remember with marketing you need to think about short-term goals, intermediate goals, and longevity. Outsmart your competition with better execution.

Wisdom

It amazes me how many individuals running a business or top managers think they know exactly what works for the company. One philosophy I believe in, is always make the time or have one of your sales people to make the time to sit with other businesses or sales people that come in to promote their product or service. In this case we will talk about advertising and marketing sales. It doesn't hurt to get the knowledge for future reference. What if they had a solution to your problems or future problems in growing business revenue. Again, I am only talking to the individuals and business who truly want to grow and change where they are currently at.

Last Thoughts

So, you're probably wondering, what do you do now? Well, I can't tell you through this book because every business has different needs and at different times, but if you schedule a consultation, in most cases, it will only take an hour for one of my team consultants or myself to tell you what you should do next. We will give you a clear road map on how to drive your business to the pinnacles that you always dreamed of. And if you would like to us to help you change gears time to time or have us on retainer, we will be glad to help. If you feel it's time to change marketing strategies, just contact us. Your business and life can change forever. If you are serious about **CUTTING THE BULLSHIT** and just getting the job **DONE**, and **GROWING YOUR BUSINESS TO GREATNESS, LET'S DO IT,**
DOMINATE YOUR COMPETITORS
CONTACT US NOW.

Resources

*Don't Forget to use promo code: CutTheBS

Marketing consulting – (Help you with entire process)

Point of Contact - Linus Ocasio

E-mail: CafeWallStreetOfficial@gmail.com

Website: www.cafewallstreet.biz

Marketing Material - (Help you with all your design and marketing material needs)

iCandy Designz, LLC

E-mail: Linus@icandydesignz.com

Website: www.icandydesignz.com

Internet Marketing – (Help you with all your internet marketing and marketing needs)

Internet Services Group Inc

Point of Contact - Drew

E-mail: Drew@spgx.net

Website: www.internetservicesgroup.net

Get Started Today

Mention Promo Discount: **CutTheBS**